grieve.
grow.
glow.

A 52-Week Guided Journey
Through Grief, Growth, and Grace

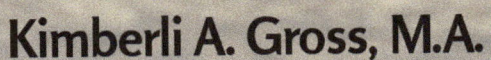

Kimberli A. Gross, M.A.

Copyright

For those learning how to live again —
without leaving love behind.

A Note From Me to You

If you're holding this booklet, I want you to know something first: there is no right way to move through grief, and there is no timeline you're supposed to be on.

I created this journal because I know what it feels like to keep living while carrying loss. I also know what it looks like to grow, rebuild, and eventually find yourself in a season where grace leads more often than grief — even though grief still shows up sometimes.

This booklet is not about getting over anything. It's about learning how to live fully in the space you're in now. Some weeks will feel lighter. Some will feel heavy. All of it is allowed.

You don't have to move through this quickly. You don't have to complete it perfectly. Take what speaks to you, sit with what challenges you, and skip what you need to.

Wherever you are as you begin, it's enough. I'm honored to walk this part of the journey with you.

How to Use This Booklet

This booklet is designed to be a companion, not a checklist.

Each week follows a gentle rhythm:

Grieve — honoring what's true.
Grow — reflecting with honesty and compassion.
Glow — practicing what supports your healing.

You don't need to rush through this rhythm or master it. Some weeks will resonate more than others, and some may feel heavier than expected. That's normal. Healing is not linear.

Throughout the booklet, you'll also find reflection weeks. These are intentional pauses — moments to look back, notice patterns, and check in with yourself. You don't need to have answers. Curiosity is enough.

There is no required start date and no set pace. If you miss a week, you haven't failed. If you linger on a page longer than planned, that's wisdom, not delay.

You may choose to work through this booklet on your own, alongside therapy, faith practices, or within a supportive community. However you engage, let it support your life — not compete with it.

Above all, be gentle with yourself.

This journey isn't about fixing grief.

It's about learning how to live with intention, honesty, and grace — one week at a time.

Just a thought...

Grief lingers, but so does grace.

Grief does not disappear because time passes. It changes shape.

Grace meets us there — not to erase grief, but to help us live alongside it.

You can grieve what was, honor what is, and still grow into what's next.

Pause here.

Notice where you are.

It's enough.

Name Your Journey

Before you begin this 52-week journey, take a moment to pause.

Grief is not a one-size-fits-all experience. What you are carrying, how it shows up, and what you need from this season may look very different from someone else's story.

This page is an invitation to name where you are—not where you think you should be.

There are no right or wrong answers here. These reflections are not meant to be final.

They may shift as you move through this book, and that's okay. Growth often begins with honesty, not certainty.

Take your time. Write what feels true right now.

_____

_____

_____

_____

_____

_____

_____

_____

_____

_____

What does *grieve* mean for me in this season?
- What loss am I carrying?
- How does my grief show up—emotionally, physically, or spiritually?
- What feels hardest to acknowledge or express?

_____

_____

_____

What does *grow* look like for me right now?
- Where do I feel stretched, unsure, or tender?
- What support, clarity, or stability do I need more of?
- What would growth not look like for me in this season?

_____

_____

_____

What might *glow* mean for me—without pressure?
- What does alignment, peace, or fullness look like right now?
- What parts of me feel ready to emerge or be nurtured?
- What am I curious about becoming, even gently?

_____

_____

_____

You don't have to rush toward these answers.
Let them meet you where you are.

When you're ready, turn the page.

Quarter 1

Grounding & Awareness

This quarter is about settling in. Before growth comes awareness.

Notice where you are without judgment. Let grace lead before expectations.

This is the foundation everything else will rest on.

Week 1: Settling In

GROW (Reflection)

This first week is not about change. It's about arrival.

Grief can make us feel like we should already be further along — more stable, more productive, more "okay." This week invites you to release that pressure. There is nothing you need to prove here.

Notice how you're showing up today — your energy, your emotions, your thoughts — without trying to improve them. Awareness is the work.

GLOW (Gentle Practice)

Pause for one minute today.
Take three slow breaths.
Quietly remind yourself: *I am here. I am safe enough to begin.*

Journal

What does "settling in" look like for me right now?

_____

Where do I feel pressure to rush myself?

_____

_____

Week 2: Allowing What's True

GROW (Reflection)

As you settle in, emotions may rise that you've learned to manage, minimize, or push aside. This week is an invitation to stop negotiating with your feelings.

Grief doesn't ask for permission to show up — and neither do the emotions that come with it. Sadness, anger, numbness, relief, gratitude, confusion — all of it can exist at the same time.

You are not weak for feeling deeply. You are human.
Let this week be about honesty, not explanation.

GLOW (Gentle Practice)

At least once this week, pause and name what you're feeling without trying to fix it.
You might say: Right now, I feel _____.
No justification required.

Journal

Which emotions feel easiest for me to allow?

_____

Which emotions do I tend to avoid or judge?

_____

_____

Week 3: Noticing What You Carry

GROW (Reflection)

By now, you may be noticing how much energy it takes just to move through the day. Grief often asks us to do invisible work — managing emotions, memories, responsibilities, and expectations all at once.

This week isn't about celebrating strength in a loud way. It's about recognizing the quiet resilience that shows up when you keep going, even while tired or uncertain.

You don't have to minimize what you're carrying to prove you're coping well. The weight matters — and so does the effort it takes to hold it.

GLOW (Gentle Practice)

Choose one moment this week to slow down and acknowledge yourself.
You might place a hand on your chest and say: This is hard, and I'm doing my best.

Journal

What feels heaviest for me right now?

_____

Where do I notice myself continuing, even when it's difficult?

_____

_____

Week 4: Pausing to Notice

GROW (Reflection)

Over the past few weeks, you've been settling in, allowing what's true, and acknowledging the effort it takes to carry what you carry. This week is not about adding anything new.
It's about noticing.

Grief work often happens quietly. Shifts don't always announce themselves. Sometimes growth shows up as awareness, language, or a softened reaction where there used to be tension.

There is no right takeaway here. Whatever you notice — clarity, resistance, exhaustion, relief — is information, not a verdict.

Let this week be gentle. Let noticing be enough.

GLOW (Gentle Practice)

Create one intentional pause this week.
Sit without distractions for a few minutes and simply observe what comes up — thoughts, emotions, sensations — without trying to direct them.

Journal

What have I noticed about myself over the past few weeks?

_____

What feels different, even in small ways?

_____

What feels the same — and how do I feel about that?

_____

Week 5: Naming What We Avoid

GROW (Reflection)

Avoidance isn't failure — it's information.

Sometimes we avoid feelings, conversations, memories, or decisions because we don't yet feel resourced enough to face them. This week invites you to notice avoidance with curiosity instead of judgment.

You don't need to force yourself into hard moments before you're ready. But you also don't have to pretend avoidance isn't there. Awareness creates choice — and choice is where growth begins.

Let honesty come first. Action can come later.

GLOW (Gentle Practice)

Notice one thing you've been avoiding emotionally or practically.
You don't have to address it yet — just name it quietly to yourself.

Journal

What have I been avoiding lately?

_____

What do I think I'm protecting myself from?

_____

What might I need in order to face this gently?

_____

Week 6: Allowing Myself to Be Seen

GROW (Reflection)

Grief can teach us how to perform strength while hiding what hurts. Over time, that performance can become exhausting.

This week invites you to notice where you hold back — where you soften your truth, minimize your needs, or keep things surface-level to avoid discomfort. Being seen doesn't mean oversharing. It means allowing honesty in spaces that feel safe enough.

You are worthy of care, not because you have it all together, but because you are human.

GLOW (Gentle Practice)

Share one honest feeling this week with someone you trust — or acknowledge it privately if that feels safer.

Journal

Where do I feel safest being honest?

_____

Where do I feel the need to hide or perform strength?

_____

What would being seen look like for me right now?

_____

_____

Week 7: Choosing What Heals

GROW (Reflection)

As awareness grows, choice begins to matter more.

This week isn't about making perfect decisions. It's about noticing where you do have agency — even in small ways. Grief can make life feel reactive, like you're constantly responding instead of choosing. Healing gently shifts that balance.

Choosing what heals doesn't always feel good in the moment. Sometimes it feels unfamiliar, awkward, or lonely. But discomfort doesn't mean you're doing something wrong. Often, it means you're doing something new.

Let this week be about intention, not intensity.

GLOW (Gentle Practice)

Notice one moment where you choose a healing response over a numbing or familiar one — even if it's small.

Journal

What choices feel most supportive to me right now?

_____

_____

Where do I default to comfort instead of care?

_____

Week 8: Pausing With Compassion

GROW (Reflection)

Over the past few weeks, you've named truth, noticed avoidance, allowed yourself to be seen, and begun choosing with more intention. That's real work — even if it doesn't feel dramatic.

This week invites you to pause and reflect without critique. You don't need to assess your progress or measure your effort. Simply notice what feels clearer, what feels tender, and what feels unchanged.

Growth doesn't always announce itself. Sometimes it shows up as awareness, language, or a softened reaction where there once was tension.

Let compassion be your lens.

GLOW (Gentle Practice)

Create a quiet moment this week to check in with yourself.
Ask gently: *What do I need more of right now?*

Journal

What feels clearer to me now than it did a few weeks ago?

_____

_____

What still feels tender or unresolved — and how do I feel about that?

_____

_____

Week 9: Noticing What Drains Me

GROW (Reflection)

As grief settles into daily life, it often shows up as exhaustion — not just physical, but emotional and mental too. This week is about noticing where your energy goes, especially in places that leave you feeling depleted or resentful.

Drained energy doesn't mean you're weak. It means something is being asked of you that may no longer fit where you are right now.

This is not a week to make big changes. It's a week to observe patterns with honesty and care.

GLOW (Gentle Practice)

At least once this week, pause and ask yourself:
What is this costing me right now?
You don't have to act — just notice.

Journal

What activities, conversations, or responsibilities feel most draining right now?

_____

_____

Where do I tend to give more than I have?

_____

_____

Week 10: Beginning to Take Up Space

GROW (Reflection)

Many people learn to survive grief by becoming smaller — quieter, easier, less demanding. Over time, this can turn into a habit of self-erasure.

This week invites you to notice where you minimize your needs, soften your truth, or stay silent to avoid inconvenience or conflict. Taking up space doesn't mean being loud or confrontational. It means allowing your presence, needs, and voice to exist without apology.

You are allowed to matter — even when it's uncomfortable.

GLOW (Gentle Practice)

Choose one moment this week to speak up, take a pause, or assert a need where you would normally stay quiet.

Journal

Where do I tend to make myself smaller?

_____

_____

What does taking up space look like for me right now?

_____

_____

Week 11: Taking Responsibility Without Self-Blame

GROW (Reflection)

As awareness grows, responsibility naturally follows — but responsibility does not mean fault.

This week is about noticing where you do have influence over your responses, patterns, and boundaries, while releasing the urge to blame yourself for what you didn't know or couldn't do at the time.

Grief often clouds clarity. Many choices were made in survival mode. That doesn't make them wrong — it makes them understandable.
Taking responsibility now is not about rewriting the past. It's about choosing differently when you're able.

GLOW (Gentle Practice)

Notice one place where you can take responsibility for your needs or reactions without criticizing yourself.
You might say: *I didn't know then. I'm learning now.*

Journal

Where do I confuse responsibility with blame?

_____

What choice feels available to me now that wasn't before?

_____

Week 13: Noticing Readiness

GRIEVE (Affirmation)

I trust my ability to notice when I am ready for what comes next.

GROW (Reflection)

Readiness doesn't always feel like confidence. Sometimes it feels like quiet knowing. Sometimes it feels like discomfort mixed with curiosity.

Over the past weeks, you've practiced awareness, honesty, reflection, and responsibility. This week invites you to notice what feels different — not because everything is resolved, but because you've built a foundation.

You may not feel eager for what's next. You may still feel cautious. Readiness doesn't require certainty. It simply asks for willingness.

Let this week be about acknowledging what you've built — even if you don't yet know how you'll use it.

GLOW (Gentle Practice)

Pause and reflect on this question:
What feels possible now that didn't feel possible before?
You don't need a full answer — just notice what comes up.

Journal

In what ways do I feel more aware or grounded than when I began?

_____

What am I carrying forward into the next season?

_____

What am I still allowed to take slowly?

_____

Looking Back Gently ~ Beginning

The past weeks may have asked more of you than you expected.

Beginning a grief journey often brings heightened awareness—of pain, of absence, of emotions that may have been waiting for space.

This pause is not about understanding everything you feel. It's about acknowledging what surfaced once you slowed down enough to notice.

Grief does not require clarity to be valid. Showing up—however imperfectly—is enough.

Take a moment to reflect on what this beginning has held.

- What felt most present as I started this journey?
- What emotions surprised me?
- Where did I feel resistance, avoidance, or hesitation?
- What felt grounding or supportive, even briefly?
- What do I need more of as I continue?

There is no right pace.
Beginning is already an act of courage.

Quarter 2
Boundaries & Responsibility

Quarter 2 is about working with what you've noticed.
With a foundation of awareness in place, this season gently shifts toward responsibility, boundaries, and choice — not as punishment or obligation, but as care. This quarter invites you to:

- take ownership of your energy and time
- notice patterns that no longer serve you
- practice boundaries without guilt
- respond with intention instead of habit

You are not expected to get this "right." Boundaries are learned through practice, not perfection.

As you move through this quarter, remember: responsibility is not about blame. It's about agency. And agency grows when you trust yourself enough to try.
Move forward at your own pace.
Let grace continue to lead.

Week 14: Redefining Responsibility

GROW (Reflection)

Responsibility has often been framed as blame — something heavy, corrective, or shaming. This week invites you to redefine it.

Taking responsibility doesn't mean you caused your grief, your loss, or the pain that followed. It means recognizing where you have influence now. It means acknowledging what you can choose, change, or release — without turning those choices into self-criticism.

Responsibility, when practiced with compassion, becomes empowerment. It's the moment you stop surviving on autopilot and begin responding with intention.

GLOW (Gentle Practice)

Identify one area of your life where you want to respond with more intention this week.
You don't need to fix it — just notice what responsibility looks like there.

Journal

How do I usually think about responsibility?

_____

Where do I feel ready to take ownership without blame?

_____

What does empowered responsibility look like for me?

_____

Week 15: Releasing What Isn't Mine

GROW (Reflection)

Grief often comes with added weight — expectations, roles, guilt, and responsibility that quietly attach themselves over time. Some of what you've been carrying may have felt necessary but no longer fits who you are now.

This week invites you to gently examine what you've taken on out of obligation, fear, or habit. Not everything you carry reflects your strength. Sometimes it reflects your kindness, your loyalty, or your desire to keep the peace.

Releasing what isn't yours doesn't mean you stop caring. It means you stop sacrificing yourself to prove that you do.

GLOW (Gentle Practice)

Notice one responsibility or emotional weight that feels heavy but misaligned. You don't have to release it yet — just acknowledge that it may not belong to you.

Journal

What responsibilities or expectations feel heaviest right now?

_____

How did I come to carry them?

_____

What might change if I allowed myself to set this down?

_____

Week 16: Letting Go of Guilt

GRIEVE (Affirmation)

I allow myself to set boundaries without carrying guilt for choosing myself.

GROW (Reflection)

Guilt often shows up when you begin to change patterns that once kept others comfortable. It can feel like a warning sign — but guilt is not always a signal that you've done something wrong. Sometimes it's simply a sign that you're doing something different.

This week invites you to notice how guilt operates in your life. Does it show up when you rest? When you say no? When you choose yourself without explaining?

Guilt doesn't mean you're selfish. It often means you're unlearning over-responsibility. Boundaries can feel uncomfortable at first — especially if you've been praised for being accommodating or strong.

Let guilt be information, not instruction.

GLOW (Gentle Practice)

When guilt arises this week, pause and ask yourself:
Is this guilt protecting my values — or my old patterns?

Journal

When do I feel guilt most strongly?

_____

What boundary feels hardest to hold without apologizing?

_____

What would self-trust look like here?

_____

Week 17: Choosing Myself Without Justification

GRIEVE (Affirmation)

I choose myself without needing to justify or defend my decisions.

GROW (Reflection)

Many people learn to survive by explaining themselves — softening decisions, offering reasons, or anticipating objections before they're spoken. Over time, this habit can quietly erode self-trust.

This week invites you to notice where you feel compelled to justify your needs, choices, or boundaries. You are allowed to make decisions that honor your capacity, even when others don't understand them.

Choosing yourself isn't rejection. It's recognition — of your limits, your values, and your worth.

You don't owe everyone an explanation for taking care of yourself.

GLOW (Gentle Practice)

Practice one moment this week where you make a choice without over-explaining. Notice how it feels in your body to let that be enough.

Journal

Where do I feel the need to explain myself most?

_____

What am I afraid will happen if I don't?

_____

What would it feel like to trust my decisions more fully?

_____

Week 18: Practicing Consistency

GROW (Reflection)

Boundaries don't become real because we name them once. They become real through repetition.

This week is about noticing how consistency feels in your body and emotions. You may feel empowered one day and uncertain the next. That doesn't mean you're doing it wrong — it means you're learning a new way of responding.

Consistency isn't rigidity. It's commitment. It's choosing to honor your needs again and again, even when old patterns try to pull you back.

Progress here is quiet, not dramatic.

GLOW (Gentle Practice)

Choose one boundary you've already identified and practice holding it consistently this week — without revisiting or renegotiating it internally.

Journal

What boundary am I practicing consistency with right now?

_____

What emotions come up when I try to hold it?

_____

What helps me stay grounded when doubt shows up?

_____

Week 19: Regulating My Emotional Responses

GROW (Reflection)

Grief and growth often stir strong emotional reactions — frustration, sadness, anger, fear. Emotional regulation doesn't mean suppressing those feelings. It means learning how to respond instead of react.

This week invites you to notice moments where emotions rise quickly. These moments are not failures — they're opportunities to practice pause, awareness, and choice.

Regulation is a skill. And like any skill, it develops through practice, not perfection.

GLOW (Gentle Practice)

When a strong emotion shows up this week, pause before responding.
Take three slow breaths and ask yourself: *What response aligns with who I'm becoming?*

Journal

What emotions feel hardest for me to regulate?

_____

How do I usually react when they show up?

_____

What support helps me respond more intentionally?

_____

Week 20: Releasing Unrealistic Expectations

GROW (Reflection)

Expectations can quietly turn into pressure—especially expectations you place on yourself. Grief changes capacity, priorities, and pace, yet many people continue to hold themselves to old standards.

This week invites you to notice which expectations feel heavy, rigid, or disconnected from where you are now. Releasing unrealistic expectations is not giving up; it's responding honestly to your current season.

You are allowed to adjust. Growth includes recalibration.

GLOW (Gentle Practice)

Identify one expectation you've been holding yourself to that feels unsustainable. Ask yourself: *Does this expectation honor who I am right now?*

Journal

What expectations feel most draining or unrealistic for me?

_____

Where did these expectations come from?

_____

What would a more compassionate standard look like?

_____

Week 21: Making Space for Disappointment

GROW (Reflection)

Disappointment is a natural part of grief and growth. It may show up when people don't meet your needs, when progress feels slower than hoped, or when life looks different than you imagined.

This week isn't about fixing disappointment or finding meaning in it immediately. It's about allowing it to exist without judgment. Disappointment doesn't mean you failed or that hope was misplaced—it means you cared.

Naming disappointment creates space for clarity and healing.

GLOW (Gentle Practice)

When disappointment arises this week, pause and name it gently:
I'm feeling disappointed because…
Let the sentence end without rushing to resolve it.

Journal

What disappointments have I been carrying quietly?

_____

How do I usually respond to disappointment?

_____

What would it look like to sit with it instead of pushing it away?

_____

Week 22: Redefining Success

GROW (Reflection)

Many people measure success by how much they accomplish, how well they perform, or how little they seem affected by hardship. Grief disrupts those measures — and invites a new definition.

This week asks you to reconsider what success looks like in this season. Success might mean setting a boundary. It might mean resting. It might mean showing up imperfectly and choosing care over appearance.

Redefining success doesn't lower the bar — it changes what the bar is measuring.

GLOW (Gentle Practice)

At the end of one day this week, name one choice that honored your well-being — even if it wouldn't look impressive to anyone else.

Journal

How have I traditionally defined success?

_____

Which measures no longer fit my life?

_____

What does success look like for me now?

_____

Week 23: Trusting My Pace

GRIEVE (Affirmation)

I trust my pace, even when it doesn't match expectations — mine or others'.

GROW (Reflection)

Grief can make time feel distorted. Some days move slowly; others feel rushed. This week invites you to step out of comparison and tune into your own rhythm.

Trusting your pace means honoring your capacity instead of fighting it. It means allowing progress to unfold without forcing timelines or milestones.

Your pace is not a problem to solve. It's information to respect.

GLOW (Gentle Practice)

Notice one moment this week where you slow down intentionally — even if it feels unfamiliar.

Journal

Where do I feel pressure to move faster or "be further along"?

_____

What happens when I allow myself to move at my own pace?

_____

What feels supportive about slowing down right now?

_____

Week 24: Reflecting on Responsibility and Boundaries

GRIEVE (Affirmation)

I honor the growth that has unfolded as I've learned to care for myself more intentionally.

GROW (Reflection)

Over the past several weeks, you've explored responsibility, boundaries, guilt, consistency, emotional regulation, expectations, disappointment, success, and pace. That's meaningful work — even if it hasn't felt dramatic.

This week is not about measuring progress or deciding whether you've "done enough." It's about noticing how your relationship with yourself may be shifting.

You may find that some boundaries feel steadier, some choices clearer, and some patterns more visible. You may also notice areas that still feel tender or unresolved. All of it belongs.

Let reflection be gentle. Integration takes time.

GLOW (Gentle Practice)

Create a quiet moment this week to reflect without agenda.
Ask yourself: *What feels different now? What still needs patience?*

Journal

What insights from this quarter feel most important to carry forward?

_____

Where do I notice growth, even if it's subtle?

_____

What do I want to approach with more compassion moving ahead?

_____

Week 25: Carrying What I've Learned Forward

GROW (Reflection)

Over the past months, you've learned how to notice your needs, set boundaries, take responsibility with compassion, and trust your pace. This week invites you to gather what feels true and supportive — not everything, just what matters most.

Integration isn't about doing more. It's about discerning what to keep. Some lessons will feel solid and ready to travel with you. Others may need more time. You don't have to force clarity.

Let this week be about intention — choosing what you want to bring with you as you continue growing.

GLOW (Gentle Practice)

Name one insight, boundary, or practice from this journey that you want to carry forward.
You might write it down or say it aloud as a quiet commitment to yourself.

Journal

What lessons from the past months feel most meaningful to me?

_____

What patterns or beliefs am I ready to leave behind?

_____

What support do I want to continue offering myself?

_____

Looking Back Gently ~ Noticing Change

By now, you may notice that grief is not static. It shifts—sometimes subtly, sometimes abruptly.

What once felt overwhelming may feel familiar, and new layers may have emerged in its place.

This pause is an invitation to notice patterns without judgment. Growth does not mean grief has disappeared. It means you are learning how to live alongside it.

Take time to reflect on what has changed—or what has stayed the same.
- What patterns am I beginning to recognize in my grief?
- Where do I notice increased awareness or capacity?
- What feels heavier than I expected at this stage?
- What tools, practices, or moments have supported me?
- What boundaries or needs am I becoming clearer about?

Growth does not require leaving grief behind.
It asks only that you notice yourself with honesty.

Quarter 3
Identity & Growth

Quarter 3 invites you to turn inward in a new way — not to revisit pain, but to reconnect with who you are becoming.

With stronger boundaries and greater self-trust in place, this season focuses on identity, values, and growth beyond survival. You may begin to notice yourself showing up differently — with more clarity, confidence, or curiosity about what's next.

This quarter is not about reinventing yourself or rushing toward a "better" version. It's about recognizing what grief has shaped, what it has clarified, and what parts of you are ready to expand.

Growth here is intentional, grounded, and rooted in self-knowledge — not urgency.
Move through this quarter with openness.
Let curiosity lead.

Let grace continue to guide you.

Week 26: Reconnecting With Myself

GRIEVE (Affirmation)

I give myself permission to reconnect with who I am now, not who I was before loss.

GROW (Reflection)

Grief can interrupt our sense of self. In the midst of surviving, you may have adapted, shifted roles, or put parts of yourself aside. This week invites you to reconnect — not to who you used to be, but to who you are becoming.

Reconnection doesn't require clarity or certainty. It begins with curiosity. You are allowed to ask questions about yourself without needing immediate answers.

This is not about reclaiming an old version of you. It's about making space for the person you are now.

GLOW (Gentle Practice)

Spend a few minutes this week doing something that feels quietly like you — even if you're not sure why.

Journal

In what ways do I feel different than I did before?

_____

What parts of myself feel unfamiliar or newly emerging?

_____

What feels worth rediscovering?

_____

Week 27: Naming What Matters to Me Now

GROW (Reflection)

Loss often clarifies what matters — not all at once, but over time. Values that once guided your decisions may shift, deepen, or fall away altogether.

This week invites you to reflect on what feels important now. Not what should matter. Not what used to matter. But what aligns with the life you're living today.

Naming values is an act of self-respect. It helps you make decisions that reflect who you are becoming, not who you feel obligated to be.

GLOW (Gentle Practice)

Choose one value that feels especially meaningful right now and notice how it shows up in your daily choices.

Journal

What values feel most present for me in this season?

_____

Which values feel less central than they once did?

_____

How do my current choices reflect what matters to me now?

_____

Week 28: Trusting My Voice

GROW (Reflection)

Grief can teach us to silence ourselves — to avoid burdening others, stirring conflict, or saying the "wrong" thing. Over time, that silence can become habitual.

This week invites you to reconnect with your voice, not as something that needs to be polished or perfect, but as something worthy of space. Your voice doesn't need to be loud to be valid. It doesn't need consensus to be true.

Trust begins when you allow yourself to speak — internally or outwardly — without editing yourself into invisibility.

GLOW (Gentle Practice)

Notice one moment this week where you pause before speaking.
Instead of holding back, allow yourself to say what feels honest — even if it's brief.

Journal

Where do I tend to silence myself?

_____

What am I afraid might happen if I speak honestly?

_____

What would trusting my voice look like right now?

_____

Week 29: Standing in Quiet Confidence

GRIEVE (Affirmation)

I allow confidence to grow quietly, without needing validation or comparison.

GROW (Reflection)

Confidence doesn't always announce itself. Sometimes it shows up as steadiness — a calmer response, a clearer boundary, or the absence of over-explaining.

This week invites you to notice where confidence is already present, even if it looks different than you expected. Confidence after grief is often quieter, deeper, and more grounded than before.

You don't need to prove your growth. You're allowed to stand in it.

GLOW (Gentle Practice)

Choose one moment this week to trust your decision without second-guessing it afterward.

Journal

Where do I already feel more confident than I used to?

_____

What does confidence look like for me now — not before?

_____

How does my body feel when I trust myself?

_____

Week 30: Allowing Myself to Be Seen

GROW (Reflection)

As you grow more comfortable with your voice and confidence, visibility may feel both inviting and unsettling. Being seen doesn't mean being fully understood or universally accepted. It means allowing your presence to exist without shrinking or hiding.

Grief can teach us to stay small to stay safe. This week invites you to gently notice where you still pull back — not to force exposure, but to recognize where safety has turned into limitation.

Being seen is not about approval. It's about authenticity.

GLOW (Gentle Practice)

Choose one situation this week where you allow yourself to show up a little more fully — without explaining or justifying who you are.

Journal

Where do I feel most comfortable being seen?

_____

Where do I still hold back, and why?

_____

What feels safe enough to share right now?

_____

Week 31: Clarifying My Purpose

GRIEVE (Affirmation)

I allow my sense of purpose to evolve as I continue to grow and heal.

GROW (Reflection)

Purpose after loss often looks different than it did before. It may feel quieter, more relational, or less tied to achievement. This week invites you to release rigid ideas of purpose and listen for what feels meaningful now.

Purpose doesn't have to be grand or fixed. It can show up in how you care, how you show up for others, or how you choose to live with intention.

Let purpose be something you notice, not something you chase.

GLOW (Gentle Practice)

Notice one moment this week that feels meaningful or aligned — even if it seems small.

Journal

What feels meaningful to me right now?

_____

How has my sense of purpose shifted over time?

_____

What feels worth nurturing in this season?

_____

Week 32: Redefining Connection

GROW (Reflection)

Grief often reshapes relationships. Some connections deepen. Others fade or feel misaligned. This week invites you to notice these shifts without forcing meaning or blame onto them.

Redefining connection doesn't mean rejecting people or closing yourself off. It means allowing relationships to meet you where you are now — not where you used to be or where others expect you to remain.

Connection that supports growth feels different than connection rooted in obligation. Learning to tell the difference is part of healing.

GLOW (Gentle Practice)

Notice one relationship this week that feels nourishing — or draining.
Simply observe how your body responds during or after that interaction.

Journal

Which relationships feel supportive in this season?

_____

Which ones feel heavier or misaligned?

_____

What do I need more of in my connections right now?

_____

Week 33: Allowing Belonging Without Losing Myself

GRIEVE (Affirmation)

I allow myself to belong without abandoning who I am.

GROW (Reflection)

Belonging after grief can feel complicated. You may want connection while also protecting the parts of yourself you've worked hard to reclaim.

This week invites you to explore belonging that doesn't require self-erasure. You are allowed to take up space, hold boundaries, and still be connected.

True belonging doesn't ask you to perform or conform. It allows you to arrive as yourself — evolving, honest, and whole.

GLOW (Gentle Practice)

Choose one interaction this week where you stay true to yourself, even if it feels slightly uncomfortable.

Journal

Where do I feel a sense of belonging right now?

_____

Where do I feel pressure to change myself to fit in?

_____

What does healthy belonging look like for me today?

_____

Week 34: Relearning Trust

GROW (Reflection)

Loss can fracture trust — in people, in life, and often in yourself. Relearning trust doesn't mean ignoring past hurt or forcing vulnerability before you're ready.

This week invites you to notice how trust shows up now. You may trust in small ways — consistency, presence, honesty — rather than in sweeping gestures or promises.

Trust is rebuilt through experience, not pressure. And it's allowed to grow slowly.

GLOW (Gentle Practice)

Notice one moment this week where you choose trust — in yourself or another — in a small, grounded way.

Journal

Where does trust feel most fragile for me?

_____

Where does it feel stronger than I expected?

_____

What helps me feel safe enough to trust?

_____

Week 35: Allowing Intimacy Without Fear

GROW (Reflection)

Intimacy after grief can feel complicated. Closeness may bring comfort, but it can also stir fear — fear of loss, disappointment, or vulnerability.t

This week invites you to explore intimacy as presence, not exposure. Intimacy doesn't require full disclosure or emotional intensity. It begins with allowing connection to exist without bracing against it.

You are allowed to open slowly. You are allowed to protect yourself and still connect.

GLOW (Gentle Practice)

Notice one moment of closeness this week — emotional or relational — and allow yourself to stay present without pulling away.

Journal

What does intimacy mean to me now?

_____

Where do I feel most comfortable being close?

_____

What fears surface around deeper connection?

_____

Week 36: Allowing Joy Without Guilt

GROW (Reflection)

Joy after grief can feel complicated. It may arrive quietly, unexpectedly, or alongside sadness. Sometimes joy brings guilt — as if feeling good means forgetting what was lost or betraying the depth of your love.

This week invites you to release that false choice. Joy does not erase grief. It exists alongside it.

Allowing joy is not denial. It's resilience. It's a sign that your heart is expanding, not forgetting.

You don't need permission to feel good. You already have it.

GLOW (Gentle Practice)

Notice one moment of joy this week — however small — and allow yourself to fully receive it without minimizing or explaining it away.

Journal

What emotions come up when I experience joy?

_____

Where do I notice guilt or hesitation around feeling good?

_____

What helps me allow joy to stay a little longer?

_____

Week 37: Making Room for Pleasure

GROW (Reflection)

Pleasure is often overlooked in grief work, yet it's deeply connected to healing. Pleasure can be sensory, emotional, creative, or relational — and it doesn't have to be extravagant to matter.

This week invites you to notice where you deny yourself pleasure out of habit, fear, or belief that it's undeserved. Pleasure doesn't require productivity. It doesn't need to serve a purpose beyond helping you feel alive.

Making room for pleasure is an act of self-connection.

GLOW (Gentle Practice)

Intentionally choose one pleasurable experience this week — something that engages your senses or brings comfort — and allow yourself to enjoy it fully.

Journal

What kinds of pleasure feel easiest for me to access?

_____

Which ones feel harder to allow — and why?

_____

How does my body respond when I give myself permission to enjoy?

_____

Week 38: Allowing Hope to Evolve

GROW (Reflection)

Hope after grief doesn't always look like excitement or certainty. Sometimes it looks like openness. Sometimes it looks like curiosity. Sometimes it's simply the belief that life can continue to hold meaning.

This week invites you to notice how your relationship with hope has changed. You may no longer hope for things to return to how they were — and that's okay. Hope can evolve without disappearing.

Allow hope to be quiet if it needs to be. Let it meet you where you are now.

GLOW (Gentle Practice)

Notice one thought or moment this week that points gently toward possibility. You don't need to act on it — just acknowledge it.

Journal

What does hope feel like for me right now?

_____

How has my understanding of hope changed over time?

_____

What makes hope feel safe or unsafe for me?

_____

Week 39: Imagining a Future With Intention

GROW (Reflection)

Imagining the future after loss can feel complicated. You may worry that looking ahead means leaving something behind. This week invites you to release that fear.

Honoring the past and imagining the future are not opposites. They can coexist. The love you carry continues — even as your life expands.

This week is not about making plans or setting goals. It's about allowing yourself to picture a future that includes growth, connection, and meaning — on your own terms.

GLOW (Gentle Practice)

Spend a few minutes imagining one aspect of your future that feels gentle, meaningful, or supportive.

Notice how it feels to let that image exist.

Journal

What feelings come up when I imagine the future?

_____

What parts of my past do I want to carry forward with me?

_____

What does a meaningful future look like for me now?

_____

Week 40: Stepping Forward With Intention

GROW (Reflection)

Moving forward doesn't mean moving on. It means choosing how you live with what you carry.

This week invites you to notice how you are already stepping forward — not through grand gestures, but through daily choices, boundaries, and presence. Intention shows up in how you respond, how you care for yourself, and how you engage with the life in front of you.

You don't have to feel fully ready to live intentionally. You only need willingness. Growth is rarely about certainty — it's about alignment.

Let this week be about noticing how far you've come and how intentionally you're showing up now.

GLOW (Gentle Practice)

Choose one small action this week that aligns with the life you want to live — not the life you think you should want.

Journal

Where do I notice intention in my daily life now?

_____

What feels aligned with who I'm becoming?

_____

What does stepping forward look like for me in this season?

_____

Looking Back Gently ~ Integration

As time passes, grief often weaves itself into daily life in quieter ways.

You may find yourself functioning more fully while still carrying loss beneath the surface.

This pause is not about measuring strength. It's about recognizing resilience—the kind that forms through endurance, self-awareness, and care.

Reflection at this stage often brings insight, even when answers remain incomplete.

- How has my relationship with grief evolved?
- Where do I notice resilience, even if I don't feel strong?
- What have I learned about myself through this process?
- What values or priorities feel clearer now?
- What am I carrying that may no longer belong to me?

You are not the same person you were when this journey began.
That does not mean you have forgotten—only that you have adapted.

Quarter 4
Integration & Living Fully

Quarter 4 is about integration — allowing everything you've learned, felt, and practiced to live alongside you as you move forward.

This season is not about perfection or arrival. It's about embodiment. You may notice yourself responding differently, trusting yourself more, or allowing joy, connection, and meaning to take up space without guilt.

Grief may still visit. That hasn't changed. What has changed is your relationship to it. This quarter invites you to live fully — not by erasing the past, but by honoring it while choosing presence, purpose, and possibility.

Let this season reflect the truth you've been building toward all along: grief lingers, but so does grace — and grace has taught you how to live.

Week 41: Living What I've Learned

GRIEVE (Affirmation)

I live from what I've learned, even when it feels imperfect or unfinished.

GROW (Reflection)

Integration doesn't happen all at once. It shows up quietly — in how you pause, how you choose, how you respond when life feels familiar or hard.

This week invites you to notice where your growth is already active. You may find yourself setting boundaries more naturally, trusting your instincts sooner, or responding with more compassion — for yourself and others.

Living what you've learned doesn't require consistency every day. It requires awareness over time. Growth isn't erased by hard moments; it's revealed by how you move through them.

GLOW (Gentle Practice)

Notice one moment this week where you respond differently than you would have in the past.
Acknowledge it — quietly and without comparison.

Journal

Where do I see my growth showing up in daily life?

_____

What feels more natural now than it used to?

_____

Where am I still practicing — and how do I feel about that?

_____

Week 42: Trusting Myself in Real Time

GROW (Reflection)

Self-trust isn't built by always getting things right. It's built by listening to yourself and responding with care — even when outcomes are uncertain.

This week invites you to notice how you make decisions in real time. Do you pause? Do you check in with yourself? Do you honor your limits?

Trusting yourself means believing you can navigate what comes — not that you'll never struggle again. It's confidence rooted in experience, not perfection.

GLOW (Gentle Practice)

Make one decision this week by checking in with yourself first.
Ask: *What feels aligned right now? — and honor the answer.*

Journal

Where does self-trust feel strongest for me now?

_____

Where do I still second-guess myself?

_____

What helps me feel grounded when making decisions?

_____

Week 43: Honoring What I Carry Forward

GRIEVE (Affirmation)

I honor the love, lessons, and strength I carry forward with me.

GROW (Reflection)

Legacy isn't only about what we leave behind for others. It's also about what we carry forward within ourselves.

This week invites you to reflect on what has shaped you — the love you've received, the wisdom you've gained, and the resilience you've built through loss. These are not burdens; they are part of your story and your becoming.

Honoring what you carry doesn't mean romanticizing pain. It means recognizing that something meaningful has taken root within you because you kept going.

GLOW (Gentle Practice)

Choose one quality, value, or lesson you carry forward and acknowledge how it shows up in your life today.

Journal

What have I carried forward from my experiences with grief and growth?

_____

Which lessons feel most important to honor?

_____

How do these show up in how I live now?

_____

Week 44: Living With Meaning

GROW (Reflection)

Meaning doesn't have to be dramatic or visible to be real. Often, it shows up in how you treat yourself, how you show up for others, and how you move through the world with awareness.

This week invites you to notice where meaning already exists in your life — not as a destination you reach, but as a way of being you practice.

Living with meaning doesn't require certainty about the future. It requires commitment to what matters now.

GLOW (Gentle Practice)

Notice one moment this week that feels meaningful — even if no one else sees it.

Journal

What gives my life meaning right now?

_____

How do I experience meaning in ordinary moments?

_____

What choices help me live with intention?

_____

Week 45: Sustaining What I've Built

GRIEVE (Affirmation)

I sustain my growth through intention, not pressure or perfection.

GROW (Reflection)

Growth isn't something you complete — it's something you tend.

This week invites you to notice what helps you stay grounded and aligned over time. Sustaining growth doesn't mean doing everything right. It means returning to what supports you when life gets busy, heavy, or unpredictable.

You don't have to recreate yourself every season. You're allowed to build rhythms that support who you are now and adjust them as needed.

Consistency here is about care, not control.

GLOW (Gentle Practice)

Identify one practice, boundary, or habit that helps you stay grounded.
Commit to revisiting it this week — gently, without expectation.

Journal

What helps me feel steady and supported?

_____

What practices feel sustainable for me long-term?

_____

Where can I simplify instead of pushing harder?

_____

Week 46: Meeting Setbacks With Grace

GROW (Reflection)

Setbacks are not signs that growth has failed. They are part of being human.

This week invites you to reflect on how you respond when things don't go as planned — when old patterns resurface, emotions feel heavier, or progress feels slower than expected.

Grace doesn't excuse harm or avoidance. It creates space to respond with honesty instead of self-criticism. You are allowed to stumble without starting over.

Growth is not erased by hard moments. It's revealed in how you meet them.

GLOW (Gentle Practice)

When a setback shows up this week, pause and offer yourself one compassionate response instead of criticism.

Journal

How do I typically respond to setbacks?

_____

What would it look like to respond with grace instead?

_____

What helps me return to myself after a hard moment?

_____

Week 47: Acknowledging How Far I've Come

GRIEVE (Affirmation)

I acknowledge my growth without minimizing the challenges it took to get here.

GROW (Reflection)

It can be hard to pause and recognize progress, especially when growth has been quiet or uneven. This week invites you to acknowledge how far you've come — not by comparing yourself to others, but by remembering where you began.

Acknowledgment doesn't require celebration or certainty. It simply asks you to see yourself clearly and honestly. Growth isn't always visible, but it is felt.

Let this week be about recognition, not evaluation.

GLOW (Gentle Practice)

Take a moment to name one way you've grown over the past year.
Hold it gently — without dismissing it or explaining it away.

Journal

Where do I notice change in myself now?

_____

What challenges did I move through that I once doubted I could?

_____

What do I want to acknowledge about my effort and resilience?

_____

Week 48: Practicing Gratitude Without Pressure

GROW (Reflection)

Gratitude after grief can feel complicated. It may coexist with sadness, longing, or unresolved pain. This week invites you to redefine gratitude — not as positivity, but as presence.

Gratitude doesn't mean everything makes sense or that loss feels acceptable. It simply means noticing what supports you now, without erasing what hurt.

You're allowed to be grateful and still grieving.

GLOW (Gentle Practice)

Notice one thing this week that supports you — a person, a moment, a resource — and acknowledge it quietly.

Journal

What does gratitude feel like for me right now?

_____

Where do I resist gratitude, and why?

_____

How can gratitude coexist with honesty in my life?

_____

Week 49: Choosing How I Live Forward

GROW (Reflection)

As this journey begins to close, the focus shifts from reflection to choice. Not because everything is resolved — but because you are more aware, more grounded, and more capable than before.

This week invites you to notice how you want to live forward. Not in a grand, permanent way, but in the daily choices that shape your life. Choice doesn't require certainty. It requires presence.

Living forward doesn't mean leaving anything behind. It means deciding how you carry what remains.

GLOW (Gentle Practice)

Identify one way you want to show up more intentionally in the coming weeks. Let it be simple, realistic, and aligned with who you are now.

Journal

How do I want to live forward from this point?

_____

What values or practices do I want to keep guiding me?

_____

What feels most important to protect or nurture?

_____

Week 50: Standing in Earned Confidence

GROW (Reflection)

Confidence at this stage isn't about certainty or fearlessness. It's about trust — trust in your ability to respond, adapt, and care for yourself when life changes again.

This confidence has been built quietly: through boundaries, reflection, choice, and compassion. It doesn't need to announce itself or prove anything.

This week invites you to acknowledge that you are not the same person you were when you began — and that growth is real, even if it still unfolds.

GLOW (Gentle Practice)

Notice one moment this week where you trust yourself without second-guessing. Allow that trust to stand on its own.

Journal

Where does confidence feel most present for me now?

_____

What experiences helped build that confidence?

_____

How does confidence feel different now than it used to?

_____

Week 51: Integrating the Journey

GRIEVE (Affirmation)

I integrate what this journey has taught me, honoring both growth and grief.

GROW (Reflection)

As this year-long journey comes to a close, this week invites you to pause and take in the whole picture. Not to summarize it neatly, but to recognize how the pieces now live together.

Integration means allowing what you've learned to become part of how you move, choose, and respond — without forcing yourself to remember every lesson or replicate every practice. Some insights will stay close. Others will resurface when needed.

You are not meant to hold this journey perfectly. You are meant to carry it wisely.

GLOW (Gentle Practice)

Create a quiet moment to reflect on the journey as a whole.
You might ask yourself: *What has changed in how I relate to myself?*

Journal

What feels most integrated into my daily life now?

_____

What lessons feel rooted, even if I don't think about them often?

_____

What do I want to continue honoring moving forward?

_____

Week 52: Living in Grace

GROW (Reflection)

This journey was never about arriving at a place where grief disappears. It was about learning how to live fully, honestly, and intentionally — even with loss in the room.

Grief may still visit. Some days may still feel heavy. And still, grace remains. Grace in how you speak to yourself. Grace in how you choose. Grace in how you live forward.

Living in grace doesn't mean you're done healing. It means you trust yourself to meet what comes with compassion, awareness, and care.

You don't outgrow grief.
You grow with it.

GLOW (Gentle Practice)

Choose one word, phrase, or intention that reflects how you want to live moving forward.
Let it guide you gently — not as a rule, but as a reminder.

Journal

What does living in grace mean to me now?

_____

How has my relationship with grief changed over time?

_____

What do I want to carry with me into the next season of my life?

_____

Looking Back Gently

Reaching this point does not mean grief has ended.

It means you have learned how to hold it with greater discernment, care, and self-trust.

This pause invites reflection on how grief now lives alongside your life—your choices, your boundaries, your sense of meaning.

There is no final version of healing. There is only continued living, informed by what you have survived.

- How do I carry grief differently now than before?
- What feels aligned in my life at this stage?
- What has grief taught me about what matters most?
- Where do I feel openness—to joy, purpose, or possibility?
- What does moving forward look like for me, on my own terms?

Grief may linger.
So does grace.

For the Road Ahead

This journey does not end here.

Grief may still visit.

Some days may still feel heavy.

And still—grace remains.

Grace in how you speak to yourself.
Grace in how you choose.
Grace in how you live forward.

May you continue to honor what you've lost while trusting what is still unfolding.
May you live with intention, compassion, and courage.
May you allow grief and growth to coexist—without apology.

Grief lingers.
But so does grace.

And grace will continue to meet you where you are.

If You're Curious About the Story

This journal was created to give you space—space to reflect, to pause, to write, and to breathe.

If, along the way, you find yourself wondering why these practices matter, or how someone else learned to live with grief and still choose growth and grace, there is a companion narrative available.

Grieve. Grow. Glow. — The Journey from Grief to Grace shares the lived experiences behind this work—the lessons, missteps, faith, and healing that shaped these pages.

You don't need to read it to complete this journal.
You don't need to read it in any particular order.
Your journey gets to be your own.

Read it alongside this journal, before it, after it, or not at all—whatever feels right for you.

And if this is where you stop, know this, the work you've done here matters.
Showing up—day by day—counts.

LICENSING LANGUAGE FOR FACILITATORS

Facilitator Use & Licensing

grieve. grow. glow. is the intellectual property of **Celebrate Still, LLC** and is licensed for use in individual and group settings under the following guidelines.

Permitted Use

Facilitators who purchase or are granted licensed access may:
- Use this booklet in facilitated group settings (in-person or virtual)
- Guide participants through weekly content at a pace appropriate for the group
- Reference and discuss affirmations, reflections, and practices during sessions
- Provide participants with their own individual copies of the booklet

Prohibited Use

Without written permission from Celebrate Still, LLC, facilitators may not:
- Reproduce, copy, scan, or distribute the booklet or its contents
- Alter, rebrand, or remove author or Celebrate Still attribution
- Record sessions for redistribution or resale
- Use the content as part of a paid program without a facilitator license

Facilitator Responsibility

This booklet is not a clinical treatment manual. Facilitators are responsible for:
- Staying within their scope of practice
- Referring participants to licensed mental health professionals when needed
- Creating emotionally safe, non-coercive environments
- Avoiding interpretation, diagnosis, or pressure to disclose personal experiences

Licensing & Permissions

For facilitator licensing, organizational use, or program partnerships, please contact:

✉ info@celebratestill.org

🌐 www.celebratestill.org

GROUP AGREEMENT / SAFE SPACE PLEDGE

Creating a Safe & Supportive Space

This group is committed to creating a space rooted in respect, compassion, and care. By participating, we agree to the following shared guidelines:

Our Commitments
- **Confidentiality:** What is shared here stays here.
- **Choice:** Sharing is always optional. Silence is respected.
- **Respect:** We honor different experiences, beliefs, and emotions.
- **No Fixing:** We listen to understand, not to advise or correct.
- **Self-Awareness:** We speak from our own experience, using "I" statements.
- **Compassion:** We approach ourselves and others with kindness, not judgment.
- **Boundaries:** We respect emotional and personal limits — our own and others'.
- **Grace:** We allow room for mistakes, learning, and growth.

What This Space Is
- A place for honesty without pressure
- A place for reflection without performance
- A place where grief and growth are both welcome

What This Space Is Not
- A place for comparison or competition
- A place for forced disclosure
- A place for minimizing pain or rushing healing

Our Shared Intention
We commit to showing up with openness, care, and respect — allowing ourselves and others to be exactly where we are.

Grief may linger, but so does grace.

About the Author

Kimberli A. Gross, M.A. is the Founder and CEO of Celebrate Still, LLC., a grief support and education organization dedicated to helping individuals and families learn how to live fully after loss.

She holds a Master's degree in Human Services Counseling with a focus on trauma, crisis response, and grief support, as well as a Bachelor's degree in Organizational Management.

This combined background allows Kimberli to understand both the emotional impact of grief and the ways people process change, meaning, and transition. Her approach is grounded, compassionate, and honest—centered on the belief that while grief does not disappear, growth, grace, and joy can exist alongside it.

Through workshops, support groups, coaching, and guided resources, Kimberli helps others build a new normal rooted in self-trust, resilience, and hope. Her work creates space for grief without rushing healing and encourages forward movement without erasing love.

Grieve. Grow. Glow. reflects both her personal journey and her professional mission: to walk with others as they learn how to carry grief—and still live.

For workshops, speaking engagements, or facilitated group experiences, email info@celebratestill.org or visit www.celebratestill.org.

Stay Connected: @celebratestill (Facebook & Instagram)